GEORGE HALL (1916-2010) ON UPPER CO

George William Hall was born on 25th October 1916 at Linsl Hall, who was a shepherd for John George Hedley, and Jane E John George Hedley. His sister Mary was born on 8th May 191! life in Upper Coquetdale. His early years were spent at Linshie 1938 the family lived at Dykeham's Edge and then at East Wilkwood until 1940. When East and West Wilkwood, like Dykeham's Edge, became artillery ranges, the family moved to Quickening Cote, later joined by George's first wife Elizabeth (1915-1970) whom he married on 14th January 1942. When the farmhouse was hit by stray shells, the family was evacuated to the huts at the Barrier. In 1952, they moved to the Peels. During his long life, Geordie did everything from shepherding and mole catching to driving caterpillar trucks but he is best known for his dry stone walls. For over seventy years, he built, renewed or repaired miles of stone wall in Upper Coquetdale.

A snapshot of Dykeham's Edge taken around 1930

"I began dry stone walling when I was eighteen. My father taught me the job and I have been building stone walls ever since. I have never had to go back to repair a wall that I have made, apart from a piece that a tractor knocked down near Carlcroft.

I grew up at Dykeham's Edge. It was a lovely farmhouse, south-facing and well sheltered from the north winds by a 12-acre wood. It was built by the Selby family as a single-storey gamekeeper's cottage. We had 25 or 30 score of sheep but just two rooms, with a byre at the end for the cows. Water came from a well and peat provided the heating. The peat fire kept the house warm in the coldest winters when snow would cut us off from the outside world. Candles or paraffin lamps provided the lighting.

There were a couple of box beds in the living room with two more in the kitchen. My father and I slept in the kitchen and my mother and sister had an iron bed in the living room. I remember that my father would often wake up during the night and light the candle so that he could sit up in bed and have a good pipe of tobacco! You could hardly catch your breath when he was having a smoke! Like East and West Wilkwood, Dykeham's Edge was last occupied around 1940 when it was cleared to make way for the artillery ranges that were expanded during the Second World War.

Our garden was small but the soil was sandy and well suited for growing carrots. We grew a few potatoes but the main crop was grown at Linshiels. In the summer, we grew a few lettuces and things for salads. It was a lonely life but we children were born into it and knew nothing else. My mother would drive geese from Linshiels to be sold at Bellingham. She would stay overnight with friends at the Dargues in Redesdale and continue to Bellingham early the next morning.

There was only a footpath from Linshiels to Dykeham's Edge. We could get snowed in for weeks and so we took care to build up a good stock of provisions. These came from Blayney's in Newcastle every six months and were delivered to Alwinton, where we collected them with the horse and cart. We would have two hundredweight bags of flour, a hundredweight bag of sugar, a big bag of salt and two gallons of whisky. Whisky was a good medicine but it also helped to pass the long winter nights!

If we felt unwell or had toothache, we either had to suffer or walk to Harbottle to get Dr. Bedford, who lived in his surgery in Hernspeth House opposite the fountain. He was the first man in Harbottle to have a car but did many of his rounds on horseback. He would come to any of the hill farms, if you sent for him. During the long winter nights, we used to play games like dominoes or whist. I used to knit socks and my sister would knit jumpers and pullovers. We got the wool from John Mowitt, who used to come round twice a year. He was known as Jack the Pack because he always carried a pack on his back with samples of clothes, such as suits, blouses and dresses. He would measure you for a new suit and get it made up. You could either pick it up from his drapery shop in Rothbury or he would deliver it on his next visit.

Mother did all the cooking with peat. We knew that 25 cartloads would last the whole winter. We built up a reserve stock in a good year in case we had a bad year and the peats got wet before they could be stored. Peat made the house very warm and we used the red peat ash on the sheep to give them a copper colour before taking them to market. We would dampen the fleece and rub the peat ash into it. After the fleece was dry, we would brush the peat out to give the fleece a lovely red colour. This was a lot of work but it was one of the tricks of the trade.

We saw a fair number of people passing by Dykeham's Edge, including large numbers of tramps. They would sleep in a byre and do odd jobs. We often met with the workers, who came to build the artillery ranges, and the soldiers, who came round once a week with the firing notices to tell us when firing would take place. Jimmy Oliver, the postman, came three days a week on Monday, Wednesday and Friday. He had lost an arm in the First World War and would walk from Harbottle to Yardhope, East and West Wilkwood, Dykeham's Edge, Quickening Cote and then back to Harbottle.

My sister Mary and I walked six miles to Harbottle School every day in all weathers. We left home at 7 o'clock in the morning and school started at 9 o'clock. It was no fun sitting in wet clothes until school finished at half past three in the afternoon! We got back home at about half past five. We went to school only in the summer. During the winter months, our mother taught us. She had been well educated herself and was an excellent teacher. She took the job very seriously and got the proper books from the school. Herbert Hearfield was the schoolmaster and he was always very pleased with our progress. One day, I remember that we had a test and I was the only one to get the right answer to one sum! On another occasion, Herbert Hearfield asked Susan Herbert the postmistress to take a couple of classes for him while he was away at a funeral. She was quite an old lady by this time and I put the school clock forward an hour without her knowing. You can imagine the reaction of Herbert Hearfield when he returned! The Anderson children at West Wilkwood had lived too far away to go to school and their mother Janet taught them everything at home.

My sister worked as a domestic maid at The Creel in Alwinton for William Dagg and his wife Catherine. Mrs. Dagg took in visitors, who came up the Coquet for the salmon fishing. Salted and dried salmon was an important part of our winter food, along with bacon and rabbits. A real delicacy was rabbit pie made with young rabbits.

My father and uncle clipped the sheep at Linshiels and Dykeham's Edge together but they would often go out and offer a day's clipping to another farm. Dry weather was essential in getting the clipping done on time. The wool from the outlying farms, such as the Ridlees and Ridleeshope, was brought down to Linbrig, where wagons would take it by road to Rothbury or Hawick.

We would drive the draft ewes to Rothbury, stay overnight and take them to the market early the next morning. It was important to have someone on hand to keep one flock separate from the next, especially as there would be a flock every fifty yards on the road between Thropton and Rothbury. One day, my father and I were driving our sheep to Rothbury. A car came in the opposite direction but, instead of waiting until the sheep went past, it kept going. The sheep were terrified and ran past the car. Father sent the dog off to stop the sheep but a bus was coming. When he met the bus, the dog went right under and out the other end. The bus meant nothing to him! He just went under the bus and stopped the sheep! We kept about four dogs: a working dog, an older one for the technical work and a couple of younger ones to take over. The older dog knew as much as you did and was good for moving the sheep along gently, without making them nervous or jump walls. The shepherds used local dogs to produce a strong working strain.

I married Bessie on 14th January 1942 and we lived at Quickening Cote with my father and mother. We soon found that Quickening Cote was in the centre of the artillery range and so every day, when firing was taking place, we were evacuated to the Barrier, between Alwinton and Linshiels, where the Army had built eighteen prefabricated huts, one for every family along the Coquet. The huts had two big rooms with proper fireplaces and boilers. We stayed at the Barrier the most because we were in the main firing line. A warden would tell us when it was safe to go back and check the farm.

It was a hard life because they were firing day and night all the year round by this time. We were going back and forth in the cold so often that Bessie got double pneumonia and had to stay in our hut at the Barrier for six weeks before she could be moved. We had some frightening experiences. One evening, we arrived back to find that a shell had landed in the room, where Bessie and I lived. It had exploded and blown all the furniture and crockery to bits. At another time, my father and I happened to be working in the sheep pens at Quickening Cote when some Canadian soldiers started to open fire at some rocks on one of the hills. But they mistook the target and one of their shells burst right over us. The shrapnel came down, just missing us but badly injuring some of the sheep that were packed into the pens.

One night, they phoned us at the Barrier and said that we could go home but that there would be some night firing. We would be fine if we stayed indoors. About midnight, they started firing over Dykeham's Edge with some of the biggest shells that they had. The whole house at Quickening Cote was shaking and a piece of shrapnel burst through the roof. I thought that we would be killed so I phoned Otterburn and eventually the firing stopped. In the end, we gave up staying at Quickening Cote altogether. It was much safer to stay in our hut at the Barrier. We were there for about eight years until we moved to the Peels in 1952. Demolition of the huts began a year after we left.

My first wife Bessie died aged 55 at the Peels on October 23rd 1970. On 31st December 1973, I married Mary Proudlock, the daughter of James Proudlock, who had been the blacksmith at the Peels, and in 1982 we moved into a new house at Townfoot in Harbottle. I carried on with building stone walls until I was 86.

I have loved being in the Coquet Valley every minute of my life and have turned my hands to many things. But I love stone-walling the most. It is nice to go round and say "I did that" and know that the stone walls that I have built will outlive me!"

CRAGSIDE   Created 1st Baron Armstrong of Cragside in 1887, Sir William Armstrong (1810-1900) built up a vast industrial and armaments complex at Elswick. In 1863, he bought 20 acres of exposed hillside near Rothbury, on which he built a modest country retreat. In 1869, he employed Richard Norman Shaw (1831-1912) to create the mansion of Cragside, the first house in the world to be lit by electricity generated by water power. This masterpiece of Victorian architecture was graced with 1,729 acres of woodland and five lakes. The once barren slopes were planted with seven million trees and shrubs and encircled by 31 miles of scenic drives and walks. Cragside stands on a plateau high above the Debdon Burn, crossed by an arched steel footbridge, 150 feet long. The estate was transferred to the National Trust in 1977 and opened for visitors two years later.

ROTHBURY   It was almost the end of the journey for these sheep as they descended Garleigh Road for Rothbury Auction Mart, opened on 21st February 1871 by Robert Donkin. Sheep would be driven for miles to be sold at Rothbury, which was one of the main auction marts for hill sheep, many of which would arrive in wagons at the adjacent railway station, the terminus of the line between Morpeth and Rothbury via Scots Gap. The branch finally closed to goods traffic on 11th November 1963 and an industrial estate now conceals all traces of the station buildings, engine shed, 42ft. turntable, sidings and platform, long enough to accommodate trains packed with people bound for Rothbury Races. Rothbury Mart became a casualty of the foot and mouth outbreak of 2001 when the cost of implementing new regulations forced the closure of older markets.

ROTHBURY Facing the medieval three-arch bridge, to which a fourth arch was added in 1759, stood the free grammar school, endowed by the Rev. Dr. John Thomlinson (1651-1720) who was rector of Rothbury for 41 years. After the foundation stone for a new school, visible on the top right of this view, was laid on 27th April 1906, plumber and ironmonger William G. Mackay (1861-1938) moved the business that he started in 1881 into the buildings of the old school. The three-storey building nearby is the Railway Hotel, one of four large hotels, which, along with boarding houses and apartments, catered for visitors, who came to enjoy the fresh air and sheltered serenity of Rothbury. Dr. Frederick Barrow (1853-1948) had a practice in High Street and maintained that Rothbury, known as the Torquay of the North, had no equal as a health resort.

8

ROTHBURY   All Saints parish church dominates Market Place, where the Armstrong Memorial, unveiled on 2nd August 1902 to Lord Armstrong and his wife Margaret, stands in front of the Newcastle Hotel. Shrouded by foliage, the tall building is Church House, a boarding house with rooms for 20 guests. After their marriage on 27th February 1919, Charles Frederick Wright (1886-1965) and his wife Ada (1888-1968) bought the business and Charles, a trained mechanic, added petrol pumps and a garage. The mansard roof of Church House was removed in 1922 and the premises became Council Offices in 1954. On the right is the Mission House, built in 1908 on the site of the old Three Half Moons Inn and now the Parish Hall. Local auctioneer Robert Donkin (1831-1914) gave the ornate street lamp to mark the coronation of Edward VII on 9th August 1902.

COUNTY HOTEL ROTHBURY. 1437

COUNTY HOTEL Within a few years of its opening, shortly before the arrival of the railway on 1st November 1870, the Rothbury Hotel had become so popular that it was renamed the County. In 1965, Sir William Leech, the millionaire Tyneside builder and philanthropist, bought the County as a holiday home for retired miners. The building was then leased to Newcastle City Council to provide similar facilities for the people of Newcastle upon Tyne. In November 1995, the Royal Air Forces Association branches in the North East purchased the County for £275,000, with the R.A.F. Association and the R.A.F. Benevolent Fund spending a further £750,000 to create a convalescent home of outstanding quality. Rothbury House opened for 36 guests on 1st July 1996 and Princess Margaret performed the formal unveiling ceremony on 8th November 1996.

"COQUET" AND RACECOURSE ROTHBURY 1916

ROTHBURY W. P. Collier has taken this view of the River Coquet and Rothbury Racecourse from behind the water pump at Pump House Corner. On the extreme left is the County Hotel, which relied heavily on racegoers, who would flock to the bar and terrace. Having hosted the annual steeplechase races on the Haugh below Carterside Farm for over 200 years, Rothbury Fields held its final meeting on Saturday 10th April 1965, with the Carterside Novices' Hurdle, the Cragside Selling Handicap Hurdle, the Rothbury Cup and the Ladies' Cup. The racecourse and its buildings, which were prone to flooding, were used by Rothbury Golf Club until an enlarged 18-hole course and new club-house were opened in March 2007. Founded in 1891, the club was originally located on elevated ground, a few hundred yards along Garleigh Road near Whitton Farm.

THROPTON Children play along the Wreigh Burn near the bridge, built in 1810. On the left stands Bridge End Cottage, behind which can be seen the tall residence of the priest of All Saints, an endowed Catholic Chapel, dating from around 1793 and enlarged in 1842. The former Presbyterian Church, with its unusual turret, was rebuilt by Frederick Wilson (1828-1894) of Alnwick in 1863 to replace an older building, dating from 1799. Church of England services are still held in the wooden mission chapel of St. Andrew, which was built in 1902. *The air here is very fresh and bracing and in the immediate vicinity, in which there are some pleasant field paths, the scenery is more typically rural than in other parts of the district. In the summer time, several of the cottages in the village are very gay with flowers.* (Jasper Salwey, Guide to Rothbury 1913)

THROPTON

THROPTON   A bus for Newcastle upon Tyne stands near the Three Wheat Heads, an 18th century inn, opposite the shop of shoemaker William Gutherson (1840-1913) who ran Thropton post office. After his death, his eldest daughter Alice became postmistress and his sons John Robert and William continued as boot and shoe makers. Tragedy struck on 14th November 1916 when their youngest brother Robert, a postman, who had joined the 7th Battalion Northumberland Fusiliers, was killed on the Somme, two days before his 34th birthday, at Butte de Warlencourt. His wife Barbara (1886-1963) opened a grocery shop and called it Warlencourt in his memory. Henry Swinburne (1869-1959) moved from Glanton in 1914 into Ord House, beside the Presbyterian Church, where he set up a garage, car hire and taxi business and ran the post office from 1926.

DAVID DIPPIE DIXON   This venerable antiquary was over 80 when his portrait was taken near Thropton post office. He became fascinated by local history while working for his father William Dixon, a grocer and draper, who had a shop in Whittingham. In 1862, he opened a shop in Rothbury for his eldest sons, David Dippie Dixon (1842-1929) and John Turnbull Dixon (1844-1926). The success of his Whittingham Vale, dating from 1887, led David to publish Upper Coquetdale in 1903, which he described as *the leisure hour employment of two village tradesmen.* Both works were illustrated by his brother, who was an accomplished artist. David was librarian to Lord Armstrong, the builder of Cragside, and to his great-nephew and heir, William Watson-Armstrong (1863-1941) who was created 1st Baron Armstrong of Bamburgh and Cragside in 1903.

HEPPLE TOWER.

861

HEPPLE TOWER Standing on private land between the former garage and shop of Charles and Adam Beattie and the Old Parsonage, built in 1888, this was one of a series of towers, built as a barrier against the Scottish Borderers. Dating from the 14th century, the great arched vault on the ground floor and the massive walls, eight feet thick, three of which still stand forty feet high, bear witness to the importance of this ancient stronghold of the lords of Hepple. The tower, which once carried battlements and turrets, was built in the troubled times before the union of England and Scotland. William Tomlinson wrote (1888) that the tower was almost demolished in the 19th century for stone to build a local farmstead *but the workmen found it easier to cut stone from the hardest quarry than to separate the massive blocks from the cement in which they were embedded.*

HEPPLE VILLAGE   850.

HEPPLE   Much of this hamlet dates from the 19th century when Sir Walter Buchanan Riddell (1810-1892) built the church, school and houses for workers on his Hepple Whitefield Estate. On the left are East Hepple cottages, with the byre at the far end now converted into a two-storey house. Opposite was Hepple forge, occupied by a series of blacksmiths, including Newton Kerr (1838-1910) and his son George (1865-1931) who are buried in the churchyard of Christ Church, consecrated on 5th July 1894. The font has a Norman bowl, found in Kirkfield, the site of an old chapel. Behind the large trees was Hepple shop and post office, which four generations of the Clark family ran between 1846 and 1962, and Hepple schoolhouse and Church of England school, which opened in 1873 for 80 children. The school closed in 1969 and is now the village hall.

SHARPERTON

SHARPERTON   Mary Clark (1860-1947) became postmistress at Hepple on the retirement of her father John on 19th April 1898 and served until she retired on 28th February 1939. Duties included taking the mail to Flotterton for delivery to Sharperton, Harbottle and Upper Coquetdale. She would have known her colleagues, spinsters like herself, Susan Herbert (1846-1931) at Harbottle and Susana Davison (1860-1940) at Sharperton. Susana Davison became postmistress on the death of her father Thomas on 3rd November 1892 and served for 48 years until her death on 10th February 1940. Sharperton Bridge opened in 1879 and was replaced in 1994. The steep gradient of Sharperton Bank was a problem for horse-drawn vehicles and passengers often had to get off and walk. Sharperton post office moved to Holystone on 24th November 1984.

HOLYSTONE.   2860.

HOLYSTONE   The church of St. Mary the Virgin stands at the heart of Holystone, the home of grocer Isabella Davidson (1826-1910) who brought up her grandsons William and Robert after their mother died on 29th August 1890. Beside the burn was Holystone Mill, where Joseph Oliver (1786-1882) and his son Joseph Hall Oliver (1830-1914) were corn millers for over eighty years. Architect Frank West Rich owned much of Holystone. He died on 25th February 1929 and his 2,790-acre Holystone Estate was auctioned on 29th July 1929 when Major Gustav Renwick (1884-1956) bought Holystone Mill and Holystone Grange. Described as the perfect English squire, he built stone kennels on the right for his greyhounds and boarded the puppies at local farms. Catherine Howey was the head teacher when the school closed on 23rd July 1965 with three pupils.

SALMON INN   The Salmon was built in the 17th century on one of the droving routes between England and Scotland. The original building was a Northumbrian long house with a cross passage where the front door now stands. A room for animals was on the right and living quarters were on the left. The original fireplace still remains with a smuggler's hole, perhaps for hiding illicit whisky from Scotland. Economic factors forced the inn to close in May 2000 and it is now a private house. W. P. Collier took this picture, which includes his motorcycle NL 3770, shortly after May 1922 when James Walsh had been succeeded as landlord by Norwich-born Robert John Wade, a retired policeman from Newcastle upon Tyne, and his wife Jane. He died aged 65 on 14th May 1936 and was succeeded by John Littlefair (1877-1973) and his wife Agnes (1881-1966).

LADY'S WELL   Tradition maintains that this spring, which supplied until 1998 the needs of Holystone, was a watering place beside the Roman road to Redesdale. It lies in a shady grove of firs, entered by a quaint gateway and now tended by the National Trust. This well, like others in Northumberland, was originally named after Saint Ninian, the fifth century apostle of the Border. The name Lady's Well was used after the first half of the 12th century when Holystone became the home of an Augustinian Priory of nuns dedicated to St. Mary the Virgin. In the centre of the oval basin of the pool is a 19th century wheel stone cross bearing the now almost illegible inscription: *In this place, Paulinus the Bishop baptised 3,000 Northumbrians, Easter DCXXVII.* Facing the spring is a statue, said to be of Paulinus, which was brought from Alnwick in 1780.

HARBOTTLE Several footbridges have been built over the Coquet to link Harbottle with the road between Alwinton and the Peels, where James Proudlock (1907-1981) was the last blacksmith. He closed his smithy in the 1950s, as tractors replaced horses, but continued to shoe horses by request for many years. Some people were afraid to use the swing footbridge, which really lived up to its name, especially children going to Harbottle School, where Herbert Hearfield (1872-1934) was the head teacher between 1905 and 1932. He was a keen photographer and recorded the destruction of an earlier bridge during the evening of 9th June 1907 when violent storms produced flash floods. He also recorded the damage at Alwinton, where the Rose & Thistle was flooded and sheep were drowned in the fields. The Coquet at Rothbury was over twelve feet above normal.

HARBOTTLE

HARBOTTLE   Overlooked by the Drake Stone, a huge boulder, 900 feet above sea level and endowed with magical powers, Harbottle consisted of one road lined with small shops. Locals are standing outside the buildings at Townfoot, where Robert Davidson (1889-1969) had his warehouse and shop. His flat cart, which brought supplies to Upper Coquetdale, has half-size wheels, a low platform, sides with bars to keep the goods secure and poles to support a canvas cover. He moved to Townhead in 1941 when both Oliver sisters died and the modern road, plans for which were first published on 10th November 1937, was built over his premises to enable motor vehicles to avoid Stables Corner, on the left, a narrow lane with a blind bend. His son James (1917-1999) continued the business after service in the R.A.F. and his marriage to Lily May Dagg on 4th October 1947.

HARBOTTLE   W. P. Collier has parked his motorcycle NL 3770 near Hernspeth House, the surgery of Godfrey Henry Bedford (1865-1942) who was the local doctor from 1902 until 1937. He was the first man in Harbottle to have a car but would ride a horse to visit the more remote farms. The Gothic fountain is the Clennell memorial, erected in August 1880 in memory of Penuel Harriet Clennell (1827-1879) of Harbottle Castle, who *devoted the powers of an active mind, the impulses of a generous heart, and the industry of a busy life to the welfare and happiness of the inhabitants of Harbottle and the neighbourhood.* In 1961, the old cottage behind the fountain was replaced by three bungalows. A boy stands outside the Star Inn, still a welcoming village hostelry, where Lionel Bootiman once brewed beer for innkeeper Gideon Pitloh in the 1860s.

23

HARBOTTLE   A lady with a pram pauses outside Huttie Cottage, the little shop of Isabel Charlton (1865-1963) and her sister Margaret (1869-1963). Children on their way home from school could buy a bagful of sweets for a farthing or two from the spinsters, who died within a week of each other. Locals could obtain almost anything they needed without leaving Harbottle but, if necessary, John Common (1848-1931) would take them to Rothbury in his horse and trap. The 1911 census includes the local Squire, his family and seven servants, the Presbyterian minister, doctor, schoolmaster, innkeeper, policeman, postmistress and letter carriers, coachman, carter, chauffeur, groom, gardener, tailor, draper, charwoman, dressmakers, gamekeepers, road repairers, grocers, boot and shoe makers, farmers, shepherds, labourers and boarding house keepers.

HARBOTTLE   Susan Herbert was postmistress of Harbottle for over 50 years and served in Border House, on the left, until a few years before she died aged 84 on 11th May 1931. She sold a wide variety of goods including the postcards of W. P. Collier, many of which would find their way straight into postcard albums. The mail arrived from Rothbury around 9.30 a.m. and was delivered by local postmen and postwomen, including Mary Tait, whose long round included Kidlandlee and the farms of the Alwin, and two soldiers of the First World War. James Oliver (1887-1953) lost an arm fighting with the King's Own Scottish Borderers and married postwoman Mary Dodd of Alwinton on 23rd June 1923. Adam Nichol (1886-1934) was a colour sergeant major in the Durham Light Infantry and married Agnes Dagg of Rookland on 27th June 1923.

HARBOTTLE This view of Townhead looks towards the former Presbyterian Church, which replaced an older building and opened on 12th July 1855. Beside the church hall, which opened in 1893, was the Foresters' Arms Inn, which closed soon after its sale to John Pitloh of the Star Inn on 21st August 1886. The door on the left led into the house and shop of Sarah Oliver (1861-1928) and her sisters Mary (1863-1941) and Margaret (1866-1941) who died within three weeks of each other. The spinsters were often seen wearing white crinoline skirts and riding their bicycles. They sold groceries, sweets and postcards and let furnished apartments. *Harbottle is much frequented during the summer months by invalids for its pure, salubrious air and the River Coquet is a favourite resort of anglers, the trout fishing being exceedingly good.* (Kelly's Directory 1914)

BARROW   This view of the Coquet Valley shows, on the right, Barrow Mill, which was used until the middle of the 19th century. The buildings are now holiday cottages and the remains of a corn drying kiln are preserved. On the left is Barrow, a three-roomed cottage with 1,092 acres of land, for nearly forty years the home of John Carruthers (1852-1934) who was a native of Hobkirk in the Scottish Borders and a shepherd at Linshiels when he married Christian Thompson on 17th March 1882. The couple moved to Hazeltonrig in 1887 and in 1894 to Barrow, owned by the Selby family of Biddlestone Hall until 30th June 1914 when H. T. Beavan (1877-1952) bought 3,468 acres of the Biddlestone Estate. John Carruthers was an area collector of subscriptions for the Coquetdale Cow Club, founded on 1st April 1882 *for the purpose of making good the loss of any cow.*

27

ANGRYHAUGH   John Carruthers retired to Angryhaugh a year before he died on 6th February 1934. Henry Thomas Beavan was the eldest son of Frederick Beavan, founder of F. Beavan Ltd, the large department store in Shields Road, Byker, which employed over 400 people. At the sale of the Biddlestone Estate, he bought Barrow & Angryhaugh and several other farms. After the death of his father on 10th October 1928, he added much of the Holystone Estate of Frank West Rich on 29th July 1929. After a cycling accident led to the death of Thomas Bland of Angryhaugh on 10th March 1943, the shop girls were allowed to take their holidays at the cottage and would meet local lads at the Rose & Thistle. In 1958, a new house was built beside the two-roomed cottage, the home of Robert Dunn of Rowhope from 1946 until his death on 19th September 1961.

ALWINTON   The modern bridge replaced this earlier bridge in 1937 when the road was levelled and widened for motor vehicles. The remains of the old bridge can be seen from Low Alwinton, which, with its loft extension and dormer windows, is now part of a modern development of holiday cottages and log cabins. Dating from Norman times, the Church of St. Michael and All Angels has 100 sittings and memorials to the Selby family of Biddlestone Hall. Ten steps lead up to the chancel floor, which was raised in the early 14th century to provide a crypt for the Clennell family. The church was renovated during the 17th and 18th centuries and was finally rebuilt in 1852 by George Pickering, the Durham architect, who rebuilt the churches at Rothbury and Holystone. On the left, the original vicarage, a larger building with fifteen rooms, is visible behind the trees.

CLENNELL HALL This was the seat of the Clennell family from the 14th century but in the 18th century it passed by marriage into the Wilkinson family. In 1880, Anthony Wilkinson (1838-1927) married Jane White (1856-1942) and used Clennell as a summer residence. In 1895, he built an extension to the left of the original house, seen covered with creeper. Anthony Wilkinson had no children and the estate passed to his nephew Clennell F. M. Drew-Wilkinson (1881-1957). The Hall became a military convalescent hospital in the Second World War. The Clennell Estate was put up for auction on 14th October 1953 but remained unsold. It was later bought by Peter Vining, who sold it to Michael T. Snaith in 1958. Clennell Hall is now a country hotel. Some of its walls are over six feet thick and Border Reivers were held in the cellars before being hanged.

ROOKLAND Facing west towards Silverton Hill and Clennell Hill, between which a track leads down to Clennell Hall, Rookland was a two-storey farmhouse, consisting of five rooms and standing in almost 1,000 acres of hill ground and pasture. Outbuildings included two byres, a calf house, pig-stye, granary and stable. In front of the farmhouse was a large paddock, enclosed by sycamore trees, and a set of clipping pens occupied a croft to the rear. Life at Rookland, which had no road access and no mains services, was hard for William and Mary Hindmarsh and their seven children, the last family to live at Rookland. They moved to Milkhope in May 1952 upon the departure of Peebles-born Andrew and Elizabeth Kirk. The clipping pens are still in use but the old farmhouse was abandoned when New Rookland was built in 1951 near the road to Biddlestone.

ROOKLAND CLIPPING   On 29th June 1872, Thomas Dagg (1852-1912) one of the five sons of Anthony Dagg of Linbrig married Agnes Rutherford (1849-1912) when she was a maid for Thomas Thompson of Bygate Hall. They had eight children but a double tragedy struck in 1912 when Agnes died on 19th March and Thomas died on 24th June. This picture, dominated by the hay stack, was taken around 1915 when their sons George and Thomas were running the farm. After service in the First World War, their brother John Dagg was at Rookland until 13th May 1940. Elizabeth, one of their sisters, stands on the right and on the left is Agnes, flanked by her cousin George Dagg of Linbrig on the right and James Smith Telfer of Rowhope on the left. On the right, the bearded George Anderson of Milkhope stands beside the kneeling James Rutherford of Singmoor.

PUNCHERTON   W. P. Collier has walked from Rookland to take this elevated view of Puncherton, now replaced by a modern house built in front of the barn. Puncherton was one of the farms of the Biddlestone Estate and consisted of 800 acres and a five-roomed farmhouse. Outbuildings included a wool house, stable, byre, pig-stye, hen house and cart shed, with a large vegetable garden and tatie field. This picture dates from around 1915, five years after James Bertram moved to Puncherton with his mother Janet, the widow of James Bertram of Bygate Hall, and his sister, also called Janet. After the death of his mother on 11th January 1916, James Bertram left Puncherton and was succeeded by William and Hannah Telfer. They were succeeded in 1921 by William and Mary Hunter, whose youngest son Richard (1929-2003) spent his whole life at Puncherton.

PUNCHERTON DIPPING   This might take place in August or September, a few weeks after clipping, when the fleece was thick enough to retain the disinfectant. The purpose of dipping was to cleanse the skin of the sheep and kill the ticks and parasites that bred disease. This picture was taken around 1913 and shows members of the Bertram family. James stands facing the camera with his nephews, Thomas sitting on the wall and Ernest standing in front of George Dagg of Linbrig, a devoted shepherd, who always wore a pocket watch in his waistcoat. They are ready to drive the sheep and lambs to be dipped by another member of the Dagg family, whose oilskins are valuable enough to be protected by the waterproof fleece apron hanging on the pen. Dipping was a family affair: the men drove the sheep while the boys gained experience in handling the lambs.

1395 BIDDLESTONE HALL.

BIDDLESTONE HALL   The Selby family rebuilt their ancestral home in 1796 and turned a pele tower into a Catholic chapel, visible on the right. Walter Charles Selby (1858-1900) was succeeded by his eldest son Walter Arthur Selby (1882-1930). He sold 8,650 acres of the Biddlestone Estate to the War Office on 31st March 1911 and put the remaining 16,994 acres up for auction on 30th June 1914. Biddlestone Hall remained unsold. By the time that this picture was taken, Walter Arthur Selby had retired to Sussex and married Dorothy Collier on 10th May 1916. Biddlestone Hall was put on sale again on 26th June 1918 and was bought by Farquhar Deuchar (1863-1947) who had inherited Deuchar's Brewery. Having been a military convalescent hospital in the Second World War, Biddlestone Hall was demolished in 1957 and only the chapel now remains.

2951   BIDDLESTONE

BIDDLESTONE VILLAGE   Having graced Biddlestone Hall with a Tuscan porch in 1796 and further alterations in 1820, the Selby family created a Georgian mansion, set within 32 acres of ornamental grounds and flanked by 215 acres of Biddlestone Home Farm. This view looks towards the village that was created to maintain an estate of over 25,000 acres. A Roman Catholic priest and housekeeper lived in the seven-roomed house on the right. On the left are six semi-detached cottages for estate workers, such as a gamekeeper, gardener, joiner, forester, woodman and stonemason. The 1891 census records Walter Charles Selby and his wife Margaret living in Biddlestone Hall, with thirteen servants and a governess for their four children, including Walter Arthur Selby aged eight, who would succeed his father, who died aged 42 on 5th March 1900.

"SINGMORE" Nº BIDDLESTONE. 787

SINGMOOR Standing in 1,255 acres of hill ground, a mile north-east of Biddlestone village, this was the four-roomed shepherd's house for Biddlestone Town Foot Farm. The gravestone of James Rutherford in Alwinton churchyard records that he was shepherd at Singmoor for 54 years. He was born on 19th October 1860 at Fairhaugh, one of the twin sons of Alexander and Jessie Rutherford, and in 1875 was living with James and Mary Young at Singmoor as their shepherd. After James died in 1887 and Mary moved into Biddlestone Town Foot Farm after her mother Margaret died on 10th April 1891, James Rutherford hired housekeepers, two of whom died at Singmoor, and spent the rest of his life at Singmoor, one of the farms of the Biddlestone Estate of the Selby family. The bachelor died in his 70th year on the farm that he loved on 6th January 1930.

ALWIN HILL MARKET   Andrew Tully of Netherton is sitting on his cart alongside Robert Davidson of Harbottle on a visit to Kidland Hill Foot in 1913. Access to isolated farms was difficult so people would meet the carrier at an agreed time and place to buy groceries or barter with eggs and butter, rabbits to feed mining villages like Ashington, or animal skins destined for furriers like Horace Friend of Wisbech. From left to right are Christian Crozier of Clennell Street, Maria Anderson of Milkhope, Isabella McLean of Kidlandlee, wearing the white hat, her mother Isabella McLean, Anthony Robson of the Heigh and his daughter Annie, Mary Ann McLean of Kidlandlee, James Rutherford, gamekeeper of Kidlandlee, and Andrew Lillico, the aged father-in-law of Anthony Robson. George Anderson, the son of Maria Anderson, stands by the horse.

KIDLANDLEE.   8qq

KIDLANDLEE SCHOOL   Plans to build a school at Kidlandlee for 20 pupils were abandoned soon after they were published on 2nd August 1911. Thomas McLean of Kidlandlee Farm was later induced to *erect a closet* in his farmhouse *for the exclusive use of a few children (8 or 10) whose parents are employed by a gentleman who has an establishment on the moors.* The schoolroom, facing the cottages on the left, welcomed nine pupils on 26th January 1914. The lives of the children were ruled by the weather, flooded fords, peats, clipping and dipping, visits by local worthies and invitations to social events at Kidland Hall. Snow forced the school to close for eight weeks during the winter of 1917. The annual school trips began in 1921 with an excursion to Bamburgh. Edinburgh was visited twice but the most popular venue was always Whitley Bay.

KIDLANDLEE SCHOOL   Williamina Bennett sits proudly with her eight pupils, all smartly dressed for the occasion, perhaps connected with the first inspection on 2nd June 1915. *This little school is in very good hands. All the work shows keen interest on the part of the Mistress and great care on the part of the scholars.* Standing, left to right, are Andrew Cowens, Ernest Bertram, Thomas Edward Cowens, George Anderson, Annie Margaret Robson and Elizabeth Annie Cowens. Alexander and Eleanor Burn Rutherford kneel in front. In 1918, Williamina Bennett took three of the girls for their first visit to Rothbury. On 30th May 1924, she retired and received a silver tea service. She returned to her native Arbroath and died aged 66 on 23rd October 1930. Elizabeth Jennings was the head teacher when the school closed on 26th July 1957 with five pupils.

PEATS Thomas McLean (1867-1942) stands outside the farmhouse of Kidlandlee, which grazed 798 Cheviot sheep on 836 acres. The peats on the cart would last about a week. After being cut in May and left to dry for a few weeks, they would be led from Peat Law, which also supplied Battleshield and Wholehope. Three generations of the McLean family were at Kidlandlee from the death of Robert Rutherford in 1856 until 1932. When the 11,816-acre Kidland Estate was put up for auction on 9th March 1925, Kidlandlee and Whiteburnshank were bought by John Thomas Lee (1874-1935) who had opened a garage and transport business in Rothbury in 1904. He kept the custom of entertaining schoolchildren at Kidland House, provided transport and pocket money for school trips and began the annual award of a gold and silver medal for the best scholars.

Clipping Sheep at Kidlandlee 899

KIDLANDLEE CLIPPING This picture of 1914 was taken from the clipping pens at Kidlandlee Farm, looking towards Kidland House, which, at 1,250 feet above sea level, dominates the skyline. This gaunt building was demolished in 1957 after standing empty for over twenty years and only the stables, visible on the left, now remain. The boy on the extreme left is Alexander Rutherford (1906-2002) who is ready to buist the sheep with tar and beside him is George Anderson (1903-1920). His father George Anderson of Milkhope stands behind Anthony Robson of the Heigh on the extreme right. The man holding the Kidlandlee mark (TK) is Henry Thompson (1872-1957) who farmed the Brigg at West Woodburn. *The entire township of Kidlandlee is let to wealthy farmers who reside elsewhere but have their shepherds living here.* (Kelly's Directory 1914)

"KIDLAND." 845.

KIDLAND HALL   Christopher John Leyland (1849-1926) would feel relieved as the final touches were being put to Kidland Hall in November 1896, though illness had postponed his final inspection of the three public rooms, fourteen bedrooms, five bathrooms, three lavatories, offices, cellars, stables and outbuildings. For over two years, the hunting, shooting and fishing Squire of Haggerston Castle had spared no expense to build the highest shooting lodge in England, with central heating throughout. The large workforce had used dynamite to blast the road up Kidland Hill and horses collapsed as they toiled up the steep slope. *It stands at a giddy altitude, considered to be the highest in the country, and very frequently may be said to be perched in cloudland, for the situation is high above the clouds some days.* (Newcastle Journal, 1st September 1896)

KIDLAND HALL W. P. Collier took this picture for his brother-in-law, Harry Ord Thompson, an established photographer of 202 Portland Road, Newcastle upon Tyne, who added his own distinctive style of titling. The two worked together between 1910 and 1912 to create a commercial collection of postcards of rural Northumberland before W. P. Collier decided to set up his own business in Bellingham. Standing under the veranda are Christopher John Leyland and his second wife, Helen Dora Cayley, whom he had married in 1892. While Haggerston Castle was being rebuilt after a disastrous fire on 5th November 1911, the couple would often stay at Kidland Hall and entertain the pupils of Kidlandlee School. On 2nd February 1914, Mrs. Bennett closed the school at 2.30 p.m. so that the children could get ready for their first afternoon tea at Kidland Hall.

MILKHOPE   South-facing and high above the Yoke Burn, the boundary between Milkhope and the Heigh, visible in the distance, Milkhope was the home of George Anderson (1859-1931) and his wife Maria (1865-1944) between 1891 and 1921. Born at Milkhope, George Anderson was a famous fiddle player but is said never to have played again after his only son George died aged 16 of measles on 7th March 1920. When the Kidland Estate was auctioned on 9th March 1925, Milkhope grazed 1,482 Blackface and Cheviot sheep on 1,733 acres. The farmhouse consisted of a living room, kitchen, larder and three bedrooms. Sheep are being gathered to the left of the gardens, fronted by rowan trees to ward off witches. Since the departure of Anthony and Jeanette Dagg in 1986, Astley Community High School has converted Milkhope into a field study centre.

THE HEIGH   Nothing now remains of this farmhouse, which consisted of three rooms, a kitchen and larder. Outbuildings included a byre, pig-stye and stable with a large paddock, where horses and sheep with weakly lambs were grazed. Peats came from Bloodybush Edge and were stacked near the sheep pens beside the house. The 1,207 acres of exposed hill land were grazed by 800 Cheviot and Blackface sheep. Anthony and Christina Robson arrived shortly before Annie, their only child, was born at the Heigh on 3rd June 1903. From 1920, the farm was the home of Robert Hall Tait and his wife Agnes, the younger daughter of George and Maria Anderson of Milkhope, and their eight children. In 1947, they were succeeded by Ella and William Potts, a noted bagpiper, and their six children. The Heigh was abandoned after their departure in May 1952.

WHITEBURNSHANK Comprising a bedroom, living room, kitchen and two lofts, this remote farm had been the home of the Murdie family for 22 years when Walter Murdie married his housekeeper Roberta Ramage on 11th November 1910. The couple overcame the loss of their sons John and Walter, who died of pneumonia on 28th and 29th April 1913, and remained on the farm of 1,009 acres and 653 Blackface sheep until 1926. After their marriage on 25th March 1942, John and Margaret Dunn became the last occupants when they moved to Kidlandlee in 1949. In 1952, John William Lee sold Whiteburnshank and Kidlandlee, once owned by his father John Thomas Lee, to the Agricultural Land Commission for afforestation and Whiteburnshank became a holiday retreat. From 1993, the Whiteburnshank Trust has maintained the farmhouse as a field study centre.

WHOLEHOPE   Standing beside Clennell Street, three miles north of Alwinton, this was one of the two cottages built for the shepherds of Shillmoor. In 1907, it became the home of James and Mary Elizabeth Cowens and their children, who attended Kidlandlee School until they moved to Philhope in 1917. From Wholehope, over 1,350 feet above sea level, the land descended towards Shillmoor and the cottage of Saughrigg, which had become unoccupied by 1871. The last shepherd at Wholehope was Edward Thompson, who left in 1942. His son George moved to North Yardhope after his marriage on 9th September 1939 to Hannah Bell Woodhall, the housekeeper that his father hired after the death of his wife Elizabeth on 4th June 1935. Wholehope opened as a basic youth hostel in 1949 but its fabric deteriorated and demolition followed after it closed in 1965.

CLENNELL STREET   The two-roomed cottage of this 800-acre hill farm was the home of Andrew and Christian Crozier between 1908 and 1923 and was part of the Clennell Estate, which was bought by Michael T. Snaith in 1958. From 12th July 1950, the land had been leased by James Waddell of Alwinton Farm but, after his death on 27th October 1967, it reverted to Clennell Hall Farm. After the death of his father in 1978, Michael J. Snaith sold the south-facing cottage, built to the east of Clennell Street, just visible at the foot of this picture. This old track over the Border runs for twelve miles from Alwinton in England to Cocklawfoot in Scotland and linked Wholehope and Whiteburnshank. Once used by pedlars, smugglers of illicit whisky, drovers and Border Reivers, this elevated route is now popular with walkers and mountain bikers.

CLIPPING SHEEP AT CLENNELL STREET. 851

CLENNELL CLIPPING Andrew Scott Crozier (1880-1957) married Christian Smith Carruthers (1885-1965) on 23rd February 1907 while working as a shepherd for his grandfather Adam Crozier at Blackblakehope in Redesdale. In his white coat, farmer and auctioneer Thomas Murray (1846-1927) of Pesspool Hall in County Durham oversees the clipping of 1915. Little Robert John Crozier (1907-1992) stands beside his father while a bearded Anthony Robson of the Heigh poses, clippers in hand, with shepherds from Whiteburnshank, Wholehope, Kidlandlee and Rookland. Clipping was hard work and required strong hands and arms but a good clipper, using hand shears, might clip 100 sheep in a day and an exceptional clipper might manage 120. Sheep were hand clipped in Upper Coquetdale until the gradual introduction of clipping machines from 1962.

ALWINTON   Until his death on 20th July 1905, the Red Lion was the inn of William Hornsby and his wife Ellen, who let rooms for visitors at 10/- per week. It then became the Temperance Hotel of Margaret Murphy. It was the boarding house of carrier and grocer Matthew Reid Wood (1874-1937) and his wife Catherine (1873-1932) in 1911 and in 1930 it became the grocery shop of John George Hedley. In 1934, Thomas and Ida Storey took over the shop, which closed in 1981. Next door is Janie's Cottage, the home of Margaret Jane Craig, who continued to run the post office, which had been in the Craig family for over forty years, after her marriage to Ralph Nichol in 1902. Her father and brother, both called John, were shoemakers and worked in the small wedge-shaped building, on the end of which Cowans & Oliver later built their village warehouse.

ALWINTON   The Hosedon Burn flows behind the wall in this picture, which looks west towards Barrow Farm, nestling beneath Barrow Hill. Bridge End Cottage is on the left and in the centre is the Rose & Thistle Inn, which remains a welcoming hostelry for locals and provides accommodation for visitors to Upper Coquetdale. Since 1852, Alwinton has hosted the Border Shepherds' Show, the last in the season, which is now held on the second Saturday in October. The newer building, near to Janie's Cottage on the right, was the warehouse of Cowans & Oliver, grocers and provision dealers, where Job Tate (1900-1985) could deliver orders for collection by local families. Despite having a cement floor, the building, which locals called the Ritz, was used for dances during the Second World War because no black-out was needed once the doors were closed.

COWANS & OLIVER William Cowans (1870-1937) moved his business into new premises at Millstone House after it was vacated by George and Mary Cummings in 1929. He opened his first shop in Rothbury when he married Isabella Gray (1868-1951) on 19th February 1896. He was born at Windyhaugh, the home of his father Robert for over forty years until his departure in 1906. James Dagg Oliver (1880-1945) was born at Cocklawfoot but lived at Uswayford after his father moved there in 1898. He married Mary Cowans, the sister of William Cowans, on 8th April 1904 and joined the business ten years later, allowing William to follow his farming interests at Cambo and Belsay. In 1932, William Cowans moved to East Green Farm, near Newmarket, where he was succeeded by his son Robert (1897-1973) and grandson William (1927-1997).

"LINBRIG" & "LINSHEELES" UPPER COQUET. 783

UPPER COQUETDALE   Having ridden a couple of miles along the road from Alwinton to Makendon, W. P. Collier has propped his bicycle against a wall at the Ducket Knowe before climbing up to take this view of Linshiels, on the left, and Linbrig, on the right. Until the opening of Linbrig Bridge in 1928, the road veered left to cross the Coquet by a ford, the first of many hazards over the next ten miles to Makendon. Many an accident occurred as carts negotiated the ford, which was wide and liable to flooding, and climbed the steep track, known as the Inch Bank, which led up from the river. Merchandise was often dislodged on the slope, much to the delight of the local lads, who would be ready to recover any lost items. It is now a broad grass track, which meets the road to the Ridlees near the semi-detached houses of New Quickening Cote.

"LINSHEELES" UPPER COQUET.

LINSHIELS   John George Hedley (1876-1954) had lived in this eight-roomed farmhouse, which was built as a shooting lodge by the Selby family of Biddlestone Hall, since 1901 when he married Olive Parr (1896-1978) on 6th December 1924. He was the first man in Upper Coquetdale to own a car, a Chevrolet, with celluloid windows. On 18th October 1916, his sister Jane Ellen Hedley married Thomas Hall, a shepherd at Quickening Cote, hidden behind the trees in the distance. The Inch Bank can be seen on the right as it climbs up from the ford across the Coquet. Pedestrians used the swing footbridge across the Coquet and a wooden bridge across the Ridlees Burn to reach Linshiels. One familiar figure would be travelling draper John Mowitt (1881-1950) of Rothbury, called Jack the Pack because of the samples that he carried on his back.

"LINBRIG"   UPPER COQUET

LINBRIG   Beneath the smoking chimney was the kitchen of Linbrig farmhouse, beside which, off the picture on the left, two semi-detached houses were built in 1953. In 1958, a metal bridge, which can easily support farm machinery and pedestrians, replaced the ford across the Coquet and the *swing footbridge of great elasticity* (Dixon). Adam Dagg (1858-1932) was born at Linbrig, married Margaret Brown (1863-1938) of Carlcroft on 29th October 1889 and took over the farm upon the death of his father Anthony ten months later. Isabella Grace Dagg (1909-1989) was the youngest of their nine surviving children and would skirt Linshiels Lake to deliver letters to the isolated farms of East and West Wilkwood before her marriage to John Hunter (1916-2003) of Puncherton on 8th July 1943. The last three members of the Dagg family left Linbrig in 1956.

LINBRIG BRIDGE   James Smith Telfer (1901-1991) was a soldier, roadman and shepherd, who worked on the new bridge from February 1927. He noted the order of bridge opening as 1st Linbrig 1928, 2nd Shillmoor 1932, 3rd Barrowburn 1933, 4th Bygate and Dumbhope 1935, 5th Rowhope, Carshope and Carlcroft 1938. The opening of the Royal Tweed Bridge at Berwick upon Tweed by the Prince of Wales on 16th May 1928 overshadowed the opening of Linbrig Bridge, which James Telfer described as a more informal affair: *Geoffrey Robson was the first man over with a car, Francis Brinton the first man with a horse and me first with a bike.* James Diggle almost drowned when a platform gave way after a flash flood and threw him into the water. Below the bridge was a salmon pool and the Linbrig tatie field, the pride and joy of the Dagg family.

QUICKENING COTE — RIDLEES BURN — UPPER COQUET — 835

QUICKENING COTE   The War Office purchased Old Quickening Cote, as the farmhouse is now called, on 7th September 1911 to be part of the new Royal Artillery Training Area. After Andrew and Margaret MacLean departed in 1923, the 970-acre farm became the home of bachelor brothers Alexander and William Crammond, who were born at the Trows, and their housekeeper. At the start of the Second World War, they were succeeded by Thomas and Jane Hall and their son George, who married Elizabeth Hall in 1942. After stray shells hit their house during practice firing, they were moved to the Barrier, where eighteen huts had been built opposite Barrow Scar between Alwinton and Linshiels. The farmhouse, now used as a troop shelter, was never occupied again and was replaced by the semi-detached houses of New Quickening Cote in 1957.

THE RIDLEES   Just a few trees and sheep pens now mark the site of this south-facing farmhouse with its nine rooms, large sundial, walled garden and stables, which had seven stalls of carved wood. Lying between Quickening Cote and Ridleeshope, the Ridlees was a farm of 6,500 acres, with five hirsels of Cheviot sheep and several shepherds, and its land provided fine hunting. David and Jane Hamilton (1923-1927) or Thomas and Agnes Dagg (1927-1938) would entertain Jacob Robson M.F.H. after he moved in 1918 from the Byrness to Coldtown Farm. He brought the Border Foxhounds with him in March and stayed for a week. Alfred Weir of Ridleeshope was the last shepherd of the Ridlees but William and Sarah Hall of Carshope lived there briefly during the winter of 1942-1943. The farmhouse gradually fell into decay and was demolished in the 1950s.

RIDLEESHOPE   This view of the two-roomed cottage and byre was taken around 1912 by John Samuel Hart, a brother-in-law of W. P. Collier. Beside the peat stack are three generations of the Robson family. The lady on the right is Isabella Robson (1843-1920) with her sons Walter and Edward and daughter Susanna with her own young daughter Isabella. Four years after their mother died aged 78 at Ridleeshope on 2nd December 1920, her sons were succeeded by Walter and Mary Cowan. In May 1926, they were succeeded by William Weir, who died aged 62 at Ridleeshope on 20th April 1933 and was succeeded by Jane and Alfred Weir, his sister and nephew. The last occupants of Ridleeshope were Robert and Mary Hutchinson, who came in 1938 but were evacuated to Toft House when artillery training increased at the start of the Second World War.

SHILLMOOR Two sportsmen walk along the road, which entered Shillmoor across a ford, a short distance from the swing footbridge. It fell out of use after a concrete road bridge replaced the ford in 1932 and was demolished in the 1960s for safety reasons. For over 100 years, Shillmoor was the home of the Ord family, first Thomas (1821-1895) and Margaret (1830-1913) and finally two of their ten children, Mary (1850-1935) and Joseph (1860-1948) who bought the 2,403-acre farm, standing at the confluence of the Coquet and Usway Burn and including the land of Saughrigg, Wholehope and Battleshield, from the Selby family on 30th June 1914. The War Office purchased Shillmoor on 19th March 1941 and built two semi-detached houses in 1953. The ten rooms of Shillmoor make it the largest farmhouse in Upper Coquetdale to be used for military purposes.

BATTLESHIELD Standing on the Usway Burn and at the foot of the peat road to Clennell Street, Battleshield was a farm of 638 acres. In 1924, it became the home of James Rutherford (1867-1959) and his wife Eleanor (1874-1962) after they moved from Kidlandlee, where James was the gamekeeper of the Kidland Estate for almost 25 years. Andrew and William, the youngest of their five children, would cross the Usway Burn and climb over Lounges Hill to go to Windyhaugh School, where their father, always known as The Keeper, was one of the managers. Clothes were washed in the burn outside the house. The small building on the Mid Hope Burn near the bridge was the first flush toilet in the area. In 1969, a new bungalow was built beside the old farmhouse, which was demolished in 2003 because of structural faults, and only the byre now remains.

HITCHY CRAG Francis Weatherston Brinton (1858-1939) was a commercial traveller, who would ride the rough road along Upper Coquetdale before improvements were made with the opening of Linbrig Bridge in 1928. For 56 years, until retiring in 1932, he worked for Blayney & Co. of Newcastle upon Tyne, a leading firm of grocers and wine & spirit merchants. Leaving his trap, known for its red wheels and shafts, at Scots Gap station, he would travel by train with his horse to Rothbury, where he would spend a week visiting his customers and taking their orders. He was so regular that people would set their clocks by him. The orders would be made up in the shop at 32 Grainger Street for local delivery. Metalled roads opened Upper Coquetdale to vans and buses and even Francis Brinton was given a motor-car with driver on 23rd April 1930.

BYGATE HALL Flitting took place on 12th May and was the traditional date when a shepherd might move from one farm to another. It was second nature to James and Mary Elizabeth Cowens, who had lived at Wholehope and Philhope before they made Bygate Hall their home between 1920 and 1937. It is said that the sole duty of one of the maids was to use peats from Fulhope Edge to stoke the seven fires in the seven rooms of the farmhouse, purchased by the War Office on 11th April 1911 along with 2,000 acres of land. Just off the picture, on the left, was a two-roomed shepherd's cottage with a cobbled courtyard, large garden and stables for four horses. Slides brought grain down from the granary above, which was once used for dances. Bygate Hall was last occupied around 1940 and was replaced in 1951 by two semi-detached houses near Bygate Bridge.

"ASKEW HALL." WINDYHAUGH. UPPER COQUET. 858

ASKEW HALL   Opened on Thursday 5th September 1935, Askew Hall was the gift of William Haggerston Askew-Robertson (1869-1942) of Castle Hills, Berwick upon Tweed, a wealthy member of the London Stock Exchange, who had the shooting rights at Uswayford. Charmed by the hospitality of local people and the fiddle playing of Archie Bertram, son of Robert and Mary Bertram of Uswayford, he had a hall built near Wedder Loup at a cost of £1,500, having personally supervised the laying of a fine wooden dance floor and presenting new violins to the five local shepherds, who played at the opening. A large marquee catered for 350 guests, who danced all night on the banks of the Coquet. For the next forty years, Askew Hall hosted many important social events but the favourite was always a whist drive and supper, followed by dancing until dawn.

WINDYHAUGH SCHOOL   A girl stands in the doorway of this remote little school, as described by a school inspector. Dating from 19th April 1879, the school was transferred to the Northumberland County Council on 3rd August 1906 and plans were finalised on 5th December 1907 to build a three-roomed schoolhouse beside Lounges Knowe farmhouse. Windyhaugh School survived threats of closure in 1946 and a new £50,000 school was built beside Askew Hall in 1971 but the end came in 1978 when the last two pupils were transferred to Harbottle School. In its 99 years, the school had just seven head teachers: Andrew Richardson Blythe (1879-1919), Mary Simpson (1919-1924), Clara Richardson (1924-1937), Elizabeth McDougle (1938-1941), Amy Trueman (1941-1955), Margaret Miller (1960-1965) and Patricia Hedley (1955-1960 and 1965-1978).

ANDREW RICHARDSON BLYTHE The son of Mary Blythe was born of Gypsy stock at Kirk Yetholm, where he had lost his left arm in a shooting incident. He trained as a teacher and, shortly after the 1871 census, arrived to teach the children of Upper Coquetdale. For over thirty years, he boarded at Windyhaugh, the farm of Robert and Eleanor Cowans, where he taught in a byre until a school was built at Lounges Knowe in 1879. Respected for his kindly disposition and sterling character, he was a great reader, firm disciplinarian and keen pipe smoker. On 6th August 1919, he received a testimonial book, inscribed with 234 names, to mark his retirement after serving for over forty years as master of Windyhaugh School. Andrew Faa Blythe, to give him his Gypsy name, was an Elder of the Kirk at Kirk Yetholm, where he died aged 82 on 19th April 1933.

WINDYHAUGH PUPILS   Clara Richardson sits with twelve of her pupils for the school photograph of April 1930 but the needs of lambing explain why several others, including John Hall of Carshope, are missing. Standing, left to right, are John Bertram of Uswayford, George Robert Wilson of the Trows, John Dunn of Rowhope, Jessie Bertram of Uswayford, William Hall of Carshope and John Drummond of Carlcroft. Seated are John Wilson of the Trows, Robert Young of Windyhaugh, Elizabeth Rutherford of Fairhaugh, Madge Bertram of Uswayford, Ernest Wilson of the Trows and William Young of Windyhaugh. George Murray of Barrowburn issued warnings of bad weather. School records mention the severe storms of winter, the Christmas party and concert, the annual trip to Whitley Bay and visits of the school inspector, nurse and dentist.

BARROWBURN The large titling makes this one of the first pictures that W. P. Collier took of Barrowburn, home to five generations of the same family since Thomas Robson (1818-1892) and his wife Eliza (1828-1902) first came to Lounges Knowe around 1860. The farmhouse is on the right with a byre, stable and pig-stye on the left. Behind the three haystacks in the field on the left are tatie pits. To the rear of the house are two peat stacks, built with peats from high above the Trows plantation. Barrowburn was the hub of Upper Coquetdale. The old road passed the farmhouse door, the Presbyterian minister held services in the kitchen or at Windyhaugh School and the teacher had a telephone in the schoolhouse and ran a small post office in the school porch. The programme of bridge and road building further along the valley did not reach Makendon until 1968.

WINDYHAUGH BARROWBURN UPPERCOQUET B15.

BARROWBURN The small titling makes this one of the last pictures that W. P. Collier took of Barrowburn, which, on the death of Andrew Robson on 26th April 1929, passed to his niece Eliza, who had married George Murray on 5th February 1927. Lounges Knowe farmhouse, described in 1921 as *unoccupied for some years and in need of repair,* is now in ruins. With the opening of the bridge at Barrowburn in 1933, a new road was built along the edge of the tatie field to replace the road through the farmyard. The new farmhouse of Barrowburn was built in 1960 to replace a temporary "terrapin" bungalow, which had been put up in 1956. The flat cart outside the old farmhouse, now used for storage, probably belongs to Robert Davidson, who visited every Wednesday and left orders at Barrowburn for collection by families at Fairhaugh and Uswayford.

BARROWBURN The history of Barrowburn revolves around its ladies. On the right is Mary Robson (1867-1951) who was the youngest daughter of Thomas and Eliza Robson. Later known as Granny Barrowburn, she had once been the local postwoman and midwife, riding her pony to the most remote farms to deliver letters or babies. On 25th March 1899, she married Edward Barton (1868-1916) and became the mother of Eliza (1900-1981) on the left. She married George Murray (1891-1979) and became the mother of Mary (1927-1989) who married Leslie Tait (1923-2009). Mary was a pupil at Windyhaugh School when she wrote about her life on a hill sheep farm. Such was the hospitality of the ladies of Barrowburn that it was considered a crime to pass the door and not go in. There was always a warm welcome and a kettle simmering on the swee.

Mary Murray (1927-1989) was the daughter of Eliza and George Murray. She became Mary Tait in March 1955 upon her marriage to Leslie Tait, from Cramlington, whom she met when he was a shepherd at Uswayford. Kindly and gentle, she lived all her days at Barrowburn, her contented life revolving around the farm, her family and children, Ian and Helen. This charming portrait of Mary, aged 10, was taken at a commercial studio during the annual Windyhaugh School trip to Whitley Bay on 20th July 1937. The children at Windyhaugh School were always very interested in what went on around them and were encouraged to record their observations in diaries. In October 1940, head teacher Elizabeth McDougle asked Mary to tell others about her life on a hill sheep farm. Recording the events of a year at Barrowburn, she writes about her mother and father, her granny, Mary Barton, and assistant shepherd, Jock Hall of Carshope, aged 24 at the time. Her words are reproduced here as they were written over 75 years ago.

MY LIFE ON A HILL SHEEP FARM

"I have the good fortune to live on a hill Sheep Farm, so I am going to try to tell others less fortunate than myself what my life is like.

The Farm on which I live is called Barrow Burn and it is surrounded by the steep Cheviot Hills, the highest of which is about six miles from here and is called Cheviot. It is 2,676 feet high. There is very little flat land round here so walking is rather difficult as, if you are not climbing up a hill, you are going down the other side.

On the Farm where I live there are over 900 acres of hill land, about 700 Cheviot sheep, 14 rams and 7 ram hoggs. We also have 3 milking cows, 2 young heifers, 1 in-calf heifer, 2 calves and 4 stirks. In the summer, we keep 2 horses, but only one in winter, as we do not have so much work. We have 30 hens, 40 pullets, 4 ducks, and 1 drake.

As neither the Farmer nor the Shepherd would be much good without his dog, we keep 5 collie dogs. Lastly, but by no means least, we have two pigs. These cause a good deal of work as a lot of food has to be prepared, such as boiled potatoes and many other things; but when they are killed and we get Bacon, Sausage, Black pudding, Potted meat, Spare rib and other such good things, we feel the work has all been worthwhile.

My life on a hill Sheep Farm is very interesting, where the work is always changing, unlike town life, where you are doing the same work day after day the whole year round. The Farmer's year begins in October when he puts the rams out on to the hill. In Winter, my Father and Jock Hall, his assistant shepherd, get up about 6 a.m., also my Mother and Grandmother. I do not get up till about 7 a.m., as I do not have a long way to walk to school, unlike most of the other children. I just have to cross the burn to go to Windyhaugh School, where there are only 9 children.

A snowstorm can be of great disadvantage to us because, if it is snowing heavily, it is not safe for most of the children to come to school. My Father depends greatly on his barometer to tell him what kind of weather there is going to be. Snow is also a great enemy of the Farmers. A snowstorm can alter his plans as to the kind of work he intended to do during the next day.

If a snowstorm happens to come through the night, this is what takes place. When my Father and Jock get up in the morning, they get their breakfast as quickly as they can. Then off they go to the hill to bring the sheep in to the stells. A stell is a fairly large round ring built of stone with an opening of about 1½ yards for the sheep to go in. They have much more shelter in the stells than if they were left out in the open, as they would get covered with snow in the drift and, through time, die of starvation. This would be a great loss to the Farmer so he tries to prevent it by putting them in stells.

A sheep dog sometimes saves a sheep's life, as some dogs are able to smell where the sheep are buried under the snow. When the shepherd sees his dog scratching away the snow, he knows that there will be some sheep there, so he digs down and, if the sheep have not been too long covered with snow, they are still alive. When the shepherd comes home and tells of what the dog has done, the dog gets a lot of petting.

After a snowstorm has continued for a few days, my Father and Jock take hay out to the sheep in a sledge. It is impossible for the sheep to get grass after the deep snow is frozen hard over the top of it. A sledge is a large oblong-shaped wooden box on two runners, pulled by a horse. Despite all its disadvantages, I rather like it when the snow is on the ground, as I go out with my sledge and come racing down the bank on it.

Water is another of the Farmer's enemies. When the snow melts and goes away, the rivers come down in flood, and some sheep either try to cross the river or stand too near the water edge. This results in them being drowned.

There are no Pictures to go to out here. So during the long winter evenings, Mother, Granny, Daddy, Jock and I all knit, and listen to the Wireless. I also do a lot of reading and a little sewing, and sometimes I go to an occasional dance and concert.

After Winter comes Spring, when all the little lambs are born. When I see the first lamb that is born trying to stand up on its wobbly legs, I feel rather glad that Winter is over at last.

Lambing time is a very busy time for all who are connected with it. My Father always gets someone to help him and Jock during the lambing time, and the last time, he got a land girl. They all go round their hills three times each day. This is done in case there should be any dead lambs or any sheep needing attention.

It is sometimes quite late when they get their work finished at night and they must be up early the next morning. If it is cold, wet weather, the weak lambs are brought in and put under cover for the night. If they were left out, they would probably die. Sometimes, when the lambs are very ill, they are brought into the house and given warm milk, and put in front of the fire. The heat from the fire, and the warm milk, revives them. If they have been too ill before they were brought in, some of them die.

After Spring is over then comes Summer. July is the month when the sheep are sheared. The shepherds from the Farms round about all go to one Farm on the same day. The day before the sheep are to be sheared at Barrow Burn, my Mother and Granny have a very busy time preparing food for all the men, who come to help to shear the sheep. I also help them as much as I can, but I cannot cook.

We all get up very early the next morning, as my Father and Jock, and all the other shepherds who have come to help them, have to collect all the sheep together and put them into sheepfolds so that they cannot get away. It generally takes nearly two days to shear our sheep or "clip" them as we call it. After the sheep have been brought in, the men all come into the house and have their breakfast.

During breakfast, the weather is a great topic of conversation as, if it starts to rain, the sheep have to be put under cover, as their fleeces must not be wet when they are clipped off. There is not always enough room for all the sheep to be put under cover, and, if it rains for a long time, the sheep do not get dry enough to be clipped that day. This means more work for the next day, and, if it rains the following day and they do not get all the sheep clipped, this means more work for the women as they have to prepare more food for another day.

When they have finished their breakfast, they start to clip the wool off the sheep. After it is all off, the sheep have an identification mark put on their right thigh. This is done by means of a steel rod with the first letter of the Farm to which they belong at the end of it. This is dipped in hot tar, and then put on to the sheep. This is called "buisting" and I sometimes do it at night, after I have come home from school. If they happen to stray away from home, people know whose sheep they are by this mark. At intervals, the shepherds go and sharpen their shears. These are like a very large pair of scissors.

After the sheep have been clipped, the fleeces are packed into large bags and sent away to Hawick later. If the men are late in being finished, they come into the house and have a meat supper but, if they are finished not long after teatime, they just have a glass of beer and a pie. There are always a lot of dishes to be washed on a clipping day.

By this time, the grass is ready to be cut and made into hay for the sheep and cattle to eat during the Winter. This is a busy time but a time that I enjoy very much.

In my Summer Holidays, Mother and I go out and work at the hay, and we sometimes have a picnic in the hay-field. If it is a sunny day, I like to have a good look round at the beautiful scenery and enjoy the sun. After the hay has all been put up in pikes, the pikes are brought in on a "bogie" which is a lot of boards of wood all nailed together forming a large oblong on two wheels, pulled by a horse. Then they are put into haystacks and hay sheds. I like to have a ride on the bogie.

In August, the lambs are taken from their mothers and sent away to be sold. Most of ours go to Wigtown. In September, the sheep are taken to a place where there is plenty of heather for them to eat. They generally stay away for about a fortnight. If they are not taken away and never get a change of food, through time they pine and die.

September is also the month when Fox hunting begins. I enjoy seeing the hounds chasing a fox and, if they are near here, I like to get out of school and see the hunt, but I cannot help feeling sorry for the poor fox when I see it being chased by so many ravenous hounds. I think Fox hunting is rather a cruel sport but, if there was none, the Foxes would get too numerous. On hunt days, we generally have a lot of people in for tea, including the Huntsman and his friends. This makes more work but we do not mind.

I hope I have succeeded in giving you a little idea of what my life on a hill Sheep Farm is like."

From the day she was born on 15th September 1927 until the day she died on 30th June 1989, Mary was a child of Barrowburn. She chose to spend the whole of her life on the farm that she loved. The words of her school essay show why she thought that Barrowburn would always be such a special place.

FAIRHAUGH   This 519-acre farm became the tenth and final addition to the Kidland Estate of Christopher John Leyland of Haggerston Castle on 11th May 1920. James Rutherford married Frances Wood on 26th March 1920 and moved into Fairhaugh as soon as the three-roomed cottage had been converted into the two-storey farmhouse, pictured on the front cover of this book. The family moved to the Sills Farm in Redesdale in 1935. A couple of cows supplied milk and two vegetable gardens produced rhubarb, potatoes, turnips and cabbages. To the right of the cottage are two haystacks and a peat stack. Lying at the foot of Fairhaugh Hill, now planted, the farmhouse was at risk from falls of snow. Sheep at Fairhaugh and Carshope were prone to pining, a lack of growth that veterinarian William Lyle Stewart discovered was caused by a lack of cobalt.

FAIRHAUGH Haymaking, clipping and dipping were times when neighbours were expected to help each other. This picture was taken near the tatie field in August 1923 and shows men from Uswayford at the Fairhaugh haymaking. The man sitting on the bogie is probably Matthew Anderson. The man standing with the hay fork is Thomas Wilson, the shepherd of Uswayford. His young son John, born in 1918, leans on the ladder. Above him stands James Rutherford of Fairhaugh. Ivie Murray, a single shepherd at Uswayford, poses on top of the stack. Frances Rutherford holds baby daughter Elizabeth, who was born at Fairhaugh on 24th April 1923. Beside her is her sister Johnina Wood, who married Ivie Murray on 20th January 1928, when the couple moved to Toft House. The stack would be left to settle, topped off with more hay and thatched with rushes.

USWAYFORD   Thomas Rennison was riding back from Alwinton and had almost reached Uswayford when he was caught in a sudden storm. George Murray later found the body of the 64-year-old shepherd on Yarnspath Law on 27th March 1914. Between 1920 and 1925, this elevated farm, with 2,063 Blackface sheep on 3,840 acres, was the home of Thomas and Robina Wilson. The farm had three haystacks and two walled vegetable gardens. Peats for the two peat stacks were led by horse and sledge from Hare Cleugh. There was a bothy for single shepherds like James Goodfellow or Ivie Murray, who were needed for such a large farm. The farmhouse had a living room, kitchen, scullery and three bedrooms. It was extended during 1946-1947 for James Dawson Telfer (1905-1974) and his family, who lived at Uswayford between 1940 and 1962.

WILSON FAMILY Shortly after their daughter Elizabeth was born at Uswayford on 6th May 1923, W. P. Collier visited Thomas and Robina Wilson to take a family portrait. Thomas, who was born at Puncherton, stands by Robina and baby Elizabeth. John, born in 1918, stands with his father and Matthew, born in 1920, stands in front of his mother. In 1924, Thomas wrote a prize essay, later published, on Herding a Hill Hirsel, a year before the family moved to the Trows, where Elizabeth died of convulsions on 24th December 1926. In 1928, the family moved to Rockey's Hall and then lived in Harbottle for a couple of years. In 1934, they made their final move to Scrainwood, where Thomas died aged 59 on 11th July 1946. *A fellow called Collier used to come around and stay in Alwinton and take photos and family pictures.* (Grace Hunter née Dagg 1909-1989)

WINDYHAUGH Robert and Eleanor Cowans let Andrew Blythe teach in one of their byres when he succeeded itinerant schoolmaster George Coulson of Simonburn, who was boarding at Fairhaugh with Alexander and Jessie Rutherford and their four children in the 1871 census. William Cowans, who was born in 1870 and later had a shop in Rothbury, was one of his first pupils and boarded his own son Robert (1897-1973) at Barrowburn to experience the teaching of his "auld Dominie." The farm was celebrated by Howard Pease (1893) in his story *The Herd of Windyhaugh,* in which a shepherd falls victim to solitude, and by Lorna Laidler (2004) in her book *Up the Valley,* in which she recalls holidays spent at Windyhaugh in the 1950s with her grandparents John and Elizabeth Nairn. The War Office purchased the 529-acre farm on 12th February 1912.

81

BARROWBURN CLIPPINGS Shepherds are making good progress with these Blackface sheep at the clipping of 1916 and the fleeces are ready to be tied, fleece side out, and loaded on to the cart or put into wool sheets, which were arranged in such a way that they became huge sacks, each holding some 60 fleeces and supplied by the firm that collected them. The girl with her head covered is probably Ellen Oliver, born in 1902, the elder daughter of Richard and Mary Oliver, who were at Windyhaugh between 1908 and 1924. She is holding a buisting iron to buist the newly clipped sheep. When she had dipped this in the tar, seen smoking behind her, she would impress the mark of Barrowburn (B inside a ring) on the sheep but would also be ready to cover any nicks made by the clippers to stop the sheep becoming infected with flies and maggots.

"ROWHOPE" UPPER COQUET 825.

ROWHOPE This view of Rowhope, which grazed 730 Blackface sheep on 1,102 acres, looks across the Rowhope Burn to the Trows. Robert Dunn moved to Rowhope after his marriage to Elizabeth Smith Telfer on 31st March 1911. His wife died in 1933 but Robert stayed on until moving to Angryhaugh in 1946. A large tatie field can be seen to the left and a half-thatched peat stack, built with peats from Black Braes. The wooden bridge led to the farm well. Between 1959 and 1975, Rowhope was the home of Hannah and Joe Hutton (1923-1995) a gentle shepherd and gifted player of the Northumbrian pipes for almost 60 years. For a further 30 years, Robert Bertram, a member of a long-established Upper Coquetdale family, continued the tradition of music at Rowhope and cutting peats. Rowhope is now farmed with the Trows and consists of almost 3,000 acres.

TROWS This six-roomed farmhouse, standing beside the Trows Burn and a huge peat stack, was the home of George and Isabella Wilson between 1928 and 1937 before they moved to Biddlestone. The whole family would be involved during May with cutting peats on Windy Gyle. It was hard work but peat was a free fuel, which burnt slowly with a hot flame and distinctive smell. After being spread out and left to dry for a few weeks, the peats were led down the peat road and carefully stacked. Poles would reduce the risk of the stack collapsing as the new peats were compressed. It was vital to build up a good reserve because periods of wet weather would make it difficult to cut new peats. The War Office purchased the Trows on 30th July 1941. In 1960, James and Mary Nairn moved from the old farmhouse into a new house, which has been unoccupied since 1978.

"CARSHOPE" UPPER COQUET.

CARSHOPE Between 1915 and 1942, this 650-acre farm was the home of William and Sarah Hall and their children, Elizabeth (Bessie) born in 1914 and twins John (Jock) and William (Wull) born in 1916. Their cousin Effie Young came in 1935 after her mother died and attended Windyhaugh School until 14th July 1940. In 1938, the Carshope ford was replaced by a bridge near the farmhouse. The girl at the door is probably Bessie, whose diaries, written between 1929 and 1934, recall the visits of Robert Davidson, John Mowitt, Henry Beavan and Francis Brinton, the arrival of a wireless on 15th May 1934 and the holidays of Charles D. Forster with his servants at Carlcroft. The family reared greyhound puppies for Major Gustav Renwick of Holystone Grange. The farmhouse became a troop shelter upon the departure of Albert and Gladys Morley in 1967.

"CARLCROFT" UPPER COQUET.   799

CARLCROFT   Charles Davison Forster (1850-1936) was a wealthy solicitor and held several important public offices in Newcastle upon Tyne. Twelve years after he became sole owner of Carlcroft, he held a grand house-warming party on 28th August 1901 to celebrate the rebuilding of the single-storey cottage as a shooting lodge. The ten rooms on the right were for his family and guests while the shepherd and his family had three rooms on the left. There were also servants' quarters. Features included a small Catholic chapel and croquet lawn. John and Ellen Oliver had Carlcroft between 1909 and 1924 and led peats from the White Rigg down the track on the left. In 1978, Jonathan Short became the first shepherd to teach the skills of upland sheep farming to the students of Kirkley Hall when the agricultural college leased Carlcroft from the Ministry of Defence.

BLINDBURN   Having failed to sell Blindburn at auction on 30th June 1914, Walter Arthur Selby accepted £12,000 on 12th February 1915 from his tenant Florence Kate Robson, widow of Thomas Robson, of Bridgeford Farm, Bellingham, for the 3,258 acres of land, an eight-roomed farmhouse, a fine range of outbuildings and the cottages of Yearning Hall and Buckham's Walls. For 23 years, Blindburn was the home of Mary Isabella Little and her husband Matthew, who died suddenly aged 70 while watching the Border Hunt on 25th January 1937. Owing to the Carshope ford being impassable to motor vehicles, his coffin was carried from Blindburn to Carshope on a farm wagon. In 1954, Blindburn ford was replaced by a bridge and two semi-detached houses were built to the east of the farmhouse. Blindburn with Makendon is now a 4,400-acre farm.

YEARNING HALL   UPPER COQUET   818.

YEARNING HALL   This view was taken from Yearning Law and looks to the Scottish Border, where Henry Rutherford Hall died aged 23 on 15th December 1874 on his return journey to Blindburn. The shepherd was found in a deep snowdrift four weeks later, his frozen hands still clutching the boots that he had collected for a friend. Two miles from Blindburn, Yearning Hall was a three-roomed cottage with a byre and pig-stye. The family gathered peats behind the cottage and kept a couple of cows. A hen house stands beside the vegetable garden. In the 1930s, Yearning Hall saw a succession of shepherds: Walter and Jane Little, Andrew and Jean Beattie and George and Gladys Lowes. The War Office purchased the farm of Blindburn and the cottages of Yearning Hall and Buckham's Walls from the Robson family on 23rd June 1941 for military training purposes.

BUCHAMS WALLS.   UPPER COQUET   835.

BUCKHAM'S WALLS   Approached by a path along the Buckham's Walls Burn or by a track along the flank of Eild Rigg, this three-roomed cottage with its tiny windows was under a mile from the Border. Peats for the huge peat stack, which fed a kitchen range and a couple of iron fireplaces, were cut from behind the house. In 1929, Buckham's Walls became the home of John Turnbull Little, his wife Margaret and their children, Elizabeth and Walter, known as Wat o' Buckham's Walls, a noted Cumberland wrestler. Winter months brought periods of isolation but Robert and Lilian Smith, who were at Makendon between 1931 and 1935, would walk over to listen to the wireless. At such an altitude, reception was excellent. Walter Little (1901-1947) continued to shepherd the west side of Buckham's Walls after the family moved to Makendon in 1941.

PHILHOPE UPPER COQUET. 795

RIVER COQUET This view of the infant River Coquet looks west towards Philhope, nestling beneath Fulhope Edge, Deel's Hill and Thirlmoor. From its source near the Roman camps of Chew Green, the Coquet takes the waters of sikes and rills to become one of the finest trout and salmon rivers. It was celebrated by Robert Roxby (1767-1846) and Thomas Doubleday (1790-1870) whose angling songs and poems were published as the Coquetdale Fishing Songs in 1852. The area teemed with sport and Walter Charles Selby of Biddlestone Hall, single-handed, in one day, once bagged 29 different head of game – fish, flesh and fowl. The demands of war, however, required land for military training and Philhope, Carshope, Linshiels, West Wilkwood and the Ridlees were the first farms to be purchased from the Biddlestone Estate on 31st March 1911.

'PHILHOPE' UPPER COQUET.

PHILHOPE W. P. Collier has climbed Fulhope Edge to take this elevated view of Philhope and the old track, which passed the farmhouse door. James and Mary Elizabeth Cowens moved from Wholehope to Philhope in 1917 before moving to Bygate Hall in 1920. On 3rd August 1921, William Little of Buchtrigg married Mary Dodd Little of Blindburn and the couple succeeded Thomas and Margaret Beck when they moved to Philhope in 1924. In 1929, they were succeeded by the sons of James and Mary Elizabeth Cowens and their wives, first James and Mary Atkinson, then Andrew and Mabel Bertram and finally Matthew Ridley and Eleanor Burn Rutherford. The modern road to Makendon climbs steeply behind the old farmhouse and peat stack. In 1955, a new house replaced the old farmhouse, which is now used for storage and the farm generator.

91

MAKENDON W. P. Collier has walked a few hundred yards south-west of Makendon, extended at the end of the 19th century, to show the isolation of this farmhouse, the last in Upper Coquetdale, flanked by the River Coquet and the frowning peaks of Thirlmoor. Between 1895 and 1918, Makendon was the home of William Weir, a single shepherd, who, like many other shepherds, would never let distance hinder attendance at Harbottle Presbyterian Church. In 1918, he moved to Dykeham's Edge and in 1926 to Ridleeshope, where he died aged 62 on 20th April 1933. Makendon saw a regular succession of occupants, including Ninian Anderson of West Wilkwood, and has been a troop shelter since 1978 when Stuart and Mary Blemings moved to Blindburn. Just over a mile away are the Roman fortifications of Chew Green and the source of the River Coquet.

EAST WILKWOOD John Samuel Hart of 95 Rothbury Terrace, Newcastle upon Tyne, a brother-in-law of W. P. Collier, took two pictures of the Wilkwoods around 1912. From 1909 to 1938, East Wilkwood was the home of John Dunn (1876-1956) and his wife Barbara (1880-1947) with their sons, John, James, Thomas, Ninian, William and Ralph. Barbara was well educated and taught the children at home because school was so far away. Three of the brothers married but none had children and the death of Ralph on 29th September 2002 ended this line of the Dunn family. With a cow byre and hen loft on the left and a stable and pig-stye on the right, this elevated farmhouse had fine views north towards the Ducket Knowe and north-west towards West Wilkwood. The Wilkwoods became one vast artillery training area on 18th March 1942 and are now in ruins.

WEST WILKWOOD   From 1855 to 1936, this was the home of Edward Anderson (1818-1906) and his second wife Janet (1834-1920) with their children, Edward, Ninian, Robert and Margaret. On 24th November 1899, Edward Anderson and William Crozier of Philhope, both in their 82nd year, were each presented with a leather easy chair. After the death of their father, Ninian (1873-1952) and Robert (1875-1934) stayed on at West Wilkwood. The brothers kept the farm beautifully but found that it was hard to get away. An exception was made for the Alwinton Show, especially in 1926, when they both received long service awards. They had a large hayrick, peat stack and walled vegetable garden. The farmhouse, which was very old and had large corner and lintel stones, looked south-east towards East Wilkwood across fields now pitted with shell craters.

UPPER COQUET   In his little shop in Bellingham, W. P. Collier has placed five separate views of Linbrig, Shillmoor, Windyhaugh, Barrowburn and Carshope in a frame and has photographed them together to produce a single multi-view postcard. On 12th June 1916, two visitors, who were on holiday at Harbottle, looked at some of his postcards and decided to walk to Windyhaugh School. The diary of their Harbottle Holiday records that they met schoolmaster Andrew Blythe and had tea at Barrowburn with Mrs. Barton. *We spoke about the school and I asked who took the sewing and great was my astonishment when she said that she did, although she said that she thought that the schoolmaster himself would have done so, had it not been that he had only one arm.* Barrowburn still extends the warmest welcome to visitors to Upper Coquetdale.

95

PURCHASE DATES OF COQUETDALE FARMS BY THE WAR OFFICE

Date	Farm	Acres	Vendor	Residence
31/03/1911	Carshope	8,650	Walter A. Selby	Biddlestone Hall
31/03/1911	Philhope	"	Walter A. Selby	Biddlestone Hall
31/03/1911	Ridlees	"	Walter A. Selby	Biddlestone Hall
31/03/1911	Linshiels	"	Walter A. Selby	Biddlestone Hall
31/03/1911	West Wilkwood	"	Walter A. Selby	Biddlestone Hall
31/03/1911	Blindburn (part)	"	Walter A. Selby	Biddlestone Hall
11/04/1911	Bygate Hall	1,991	Ralph H. Carr-Ellison	Hedgeley Hall
11/04/1911	Makendon	683	Ralph H. Carr-Ellison	Hedgeley Hall
07/09/1911	Quickening Cote	970	George Dunn	Berkshire
12/02/1912	Windyhaugh	529	William H. Pawson	Titlington Hall
19/03/1941	Battleshield	637	J. O. & F. R. Ord	Shillmoor
19/03/1941	Shillmoor	1,030	J. O. & F. R. Ord	Shillmoor
19/03/1941	Wholehope	736	J. O. & F. R. Ord	Shillmoor
22/05/1941	Rowhope	1,102	George Anderson	Cambo
23/06/1941	Blindburn	3,258	Florence K. Robson	Bellingham
18/07/1941	Linbrig	1,190	Elizabeth Eyston	Berkshire
			[sister of George Dunn who died in 1912]	
30/07/1941	Trows	1,600	Robert Rickelton	Glanton
06/03/1942	Barrowburn	929	Mary A. Barton	Barrowburn
06/03/1942	Lounges Knowe	"	Mary A. Barton	Barrowburn
18/03/1942	Barrow (land)	3,230	Henry T. Beavan	Shawdon Hall
18/03/1942	Linshiels (land)	"	Henry T. Beavan	Shawdon Hall
18/03/1942	West Wilkwood (land)	"	Henry T. Beavan	Shawdon Hall
18/03/1942	East Wilkwood (land)	"	Henry T. Beavan	Shawdon Hall
28/01/1943	Carlcroft (land)	1,270	Charles D. Forster	[died in 1936]
07/09/1953	Barrow & Angryhaugh	310	Henry T. Beavan	[died in 1952]